CW01261802

MAMMALS OF THE AFRICAN SAVANNA

Animal Book 2nd Grade Children's Animal Books

BABY PROFESSOR
EDUCATION KIDS

Speedy Publishing LLC
40 E. Main St. #1156
Newark, DE 19711
www.speedypublishing.com
Copyright 2017

All Rights reserved. No part of this book may be reproduced or used in any way or form or by any means whether electronic or mechanical, this means that you cannot record or photocopy any material ideas or tips that are provided in this book.

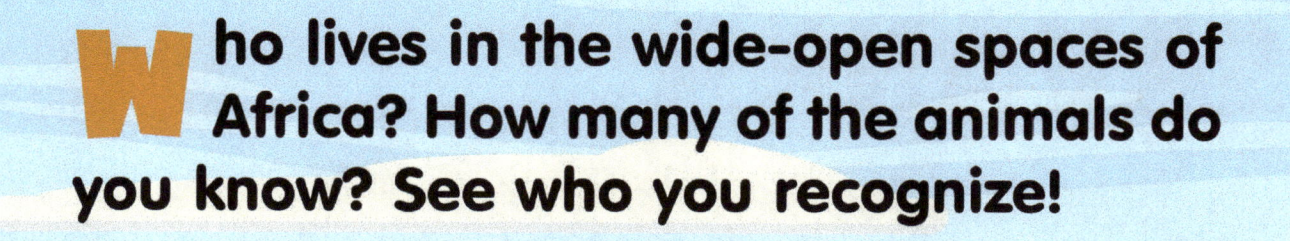

Who lives in the wide-open spaces of Africa? How many of the animals do you know? See who you recognize!

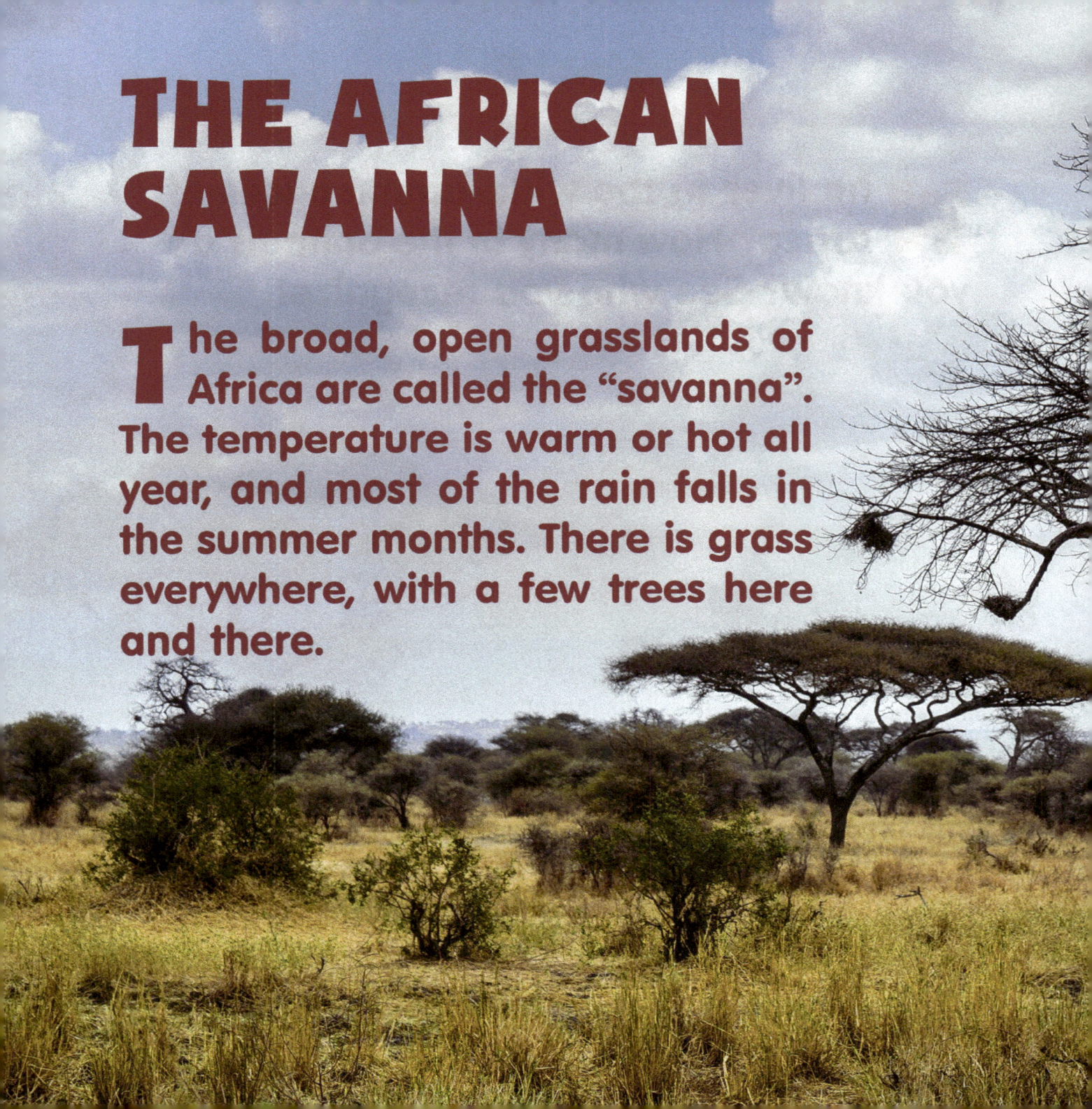

THE AFRICAN SAVANNA

The broad, open grasslands of Africa are called the "savanna". The temperature is warm or hot all year, and most of the rain falls in the summer months. There is grass everywhere, with a few trees here and there.

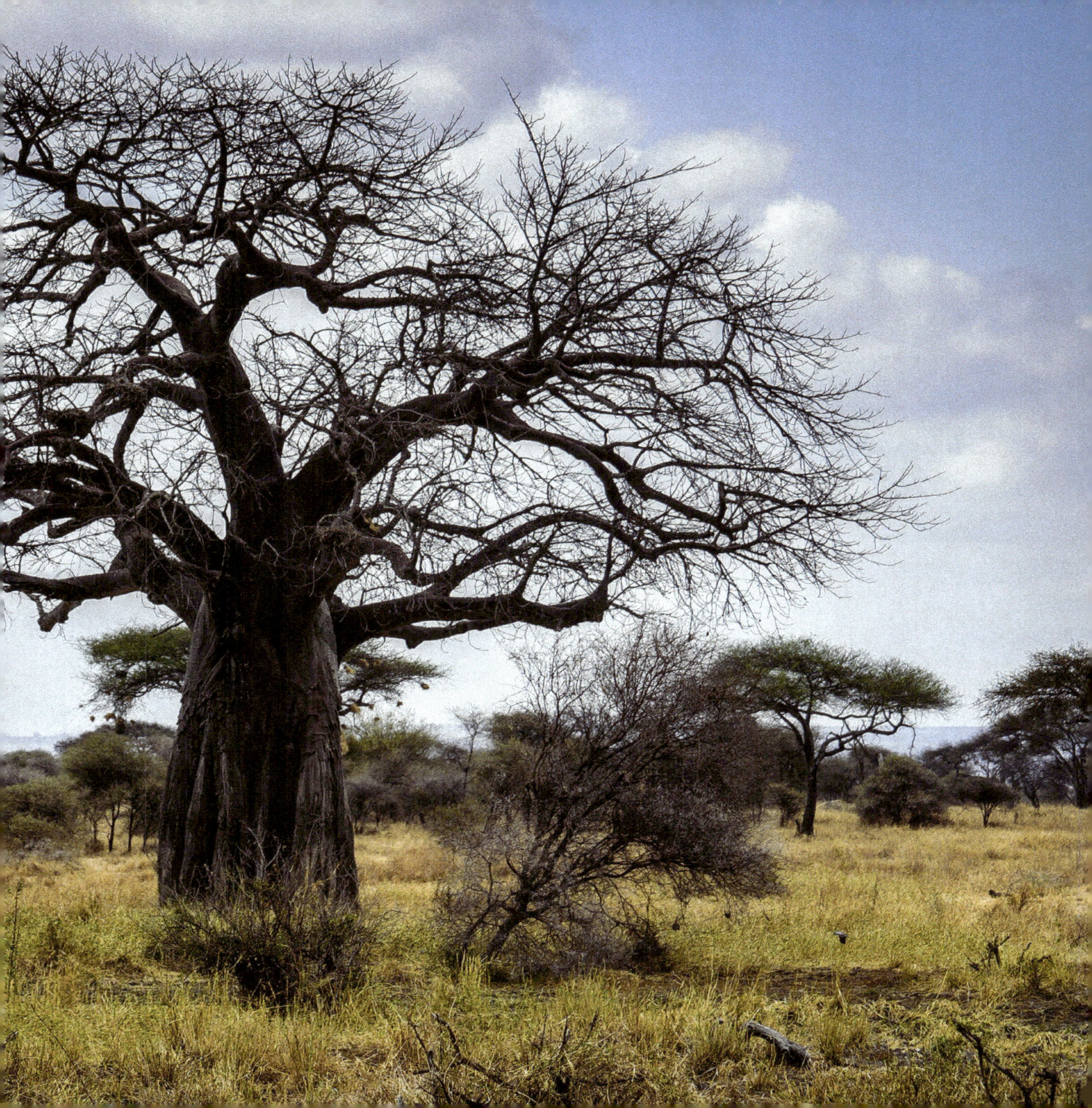

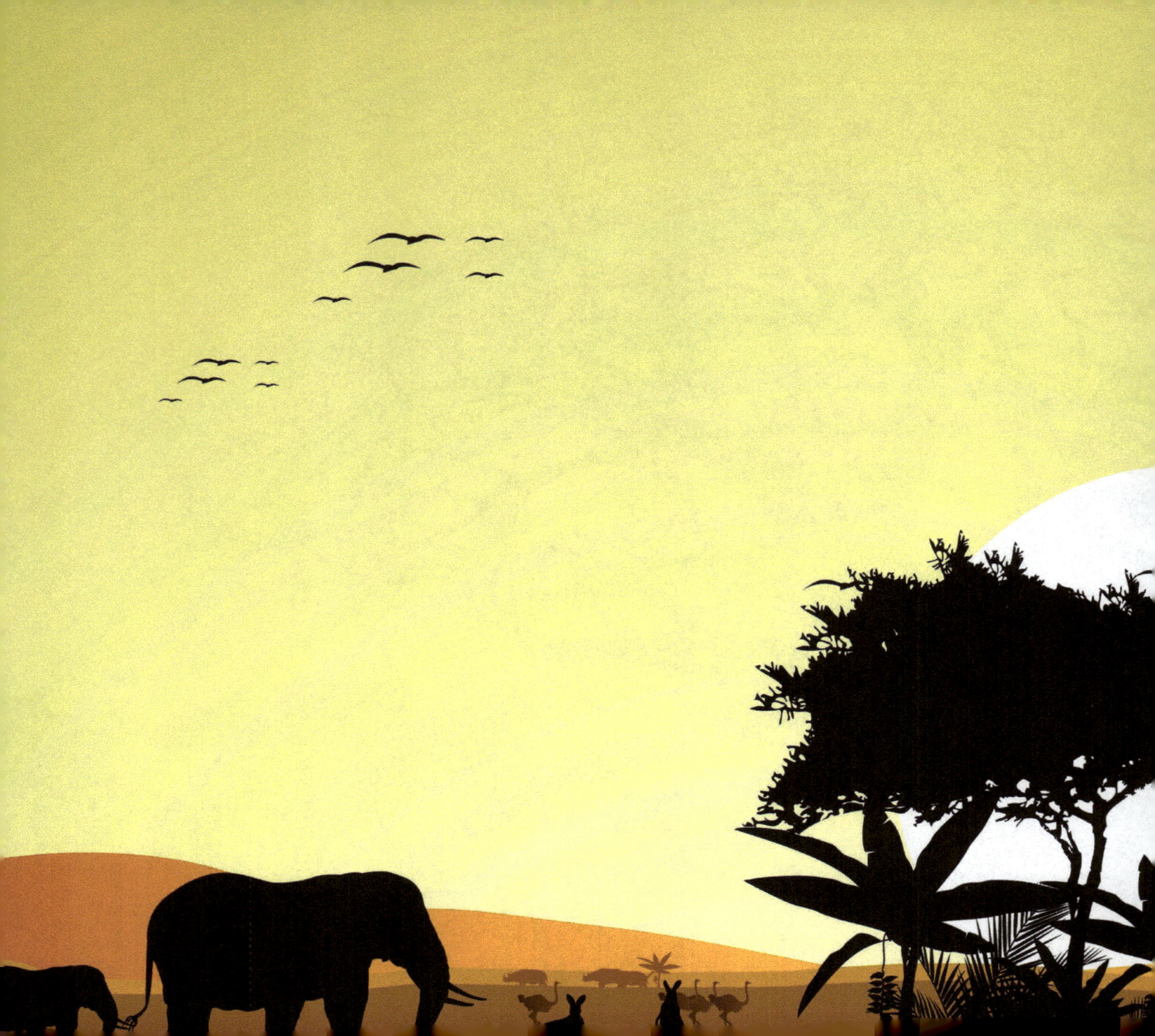

And you know what else is everywhere in the savanna? Animals! There are birds and lizards and snakes, but let's concentrate for now on the mammals. Mammals are warm-blooded, give birth to live babies instead of eggs that have to hatch, and the mothers give milk to their babies as they are growing.

Mammals have a lot in common. But there are a lot of differences, too. Let's see what mammals we can find on the African savanna!

HUNTERS

There are savanna animals that hunt and eat other animals. They have to be fast and smart, with excellent hearing and eyesight. Here are some:

CARACAL

These hunters are also known as lynx cats. They are great jumpers, and can jump high in the air to catch passing birds. Most of the time they hunt small animals like mice and rabbits, and small antelopes.

YOUNG CARACAL IN A HOLE IN A TREE TRUNK

WILD AFRICAN CHEETAH

CHEETAH

They are very fast hunting cats. They can go from standing still to over fifty miles an hour in about three seconds! As the savanna gets smaller, the cheetahs have fewer opportunities to hunt, and they are in danger of becoming extinct.

HYENA

People used to think that hyenas only ate what was left from what other animals killed. But it is not true. They are very intelligent hunters who work together to isolate and bring down an animal they have selected. A pack of hyenas can even take on large targets like buffalo.

HYENA

BLACK-BACKED JACKAL

JACKAL

Jackals will eat almost anything they can catch, and they also are quick to eat what other animals have killed and left behind.

LEOPARD

Leopards work alone, and usually hunt at night. They are very good at climbing, so even animals up trees or rocky slopes are not safe from them.

LEOPARD LYING IN GRASS

AFRICAN LION IN THE SAVANNA

LION

Lions live in prides, with one male in charge and many females and some younger males. Lions have excellent night vision, so they like to hunt then. Most of the hunting is done by groups of females.

HERD ANIMALS

The savanna is a broad grassland, so there are a lot of grass-eating animals, as well as animals that eat leaves and fruit from the occasional tree. They move slowly from area to area, chewing their way across Africa. Grass-eaters tend to live and move in herds, large groups of the same type of animal.

Do you know these savanna grass eaters?

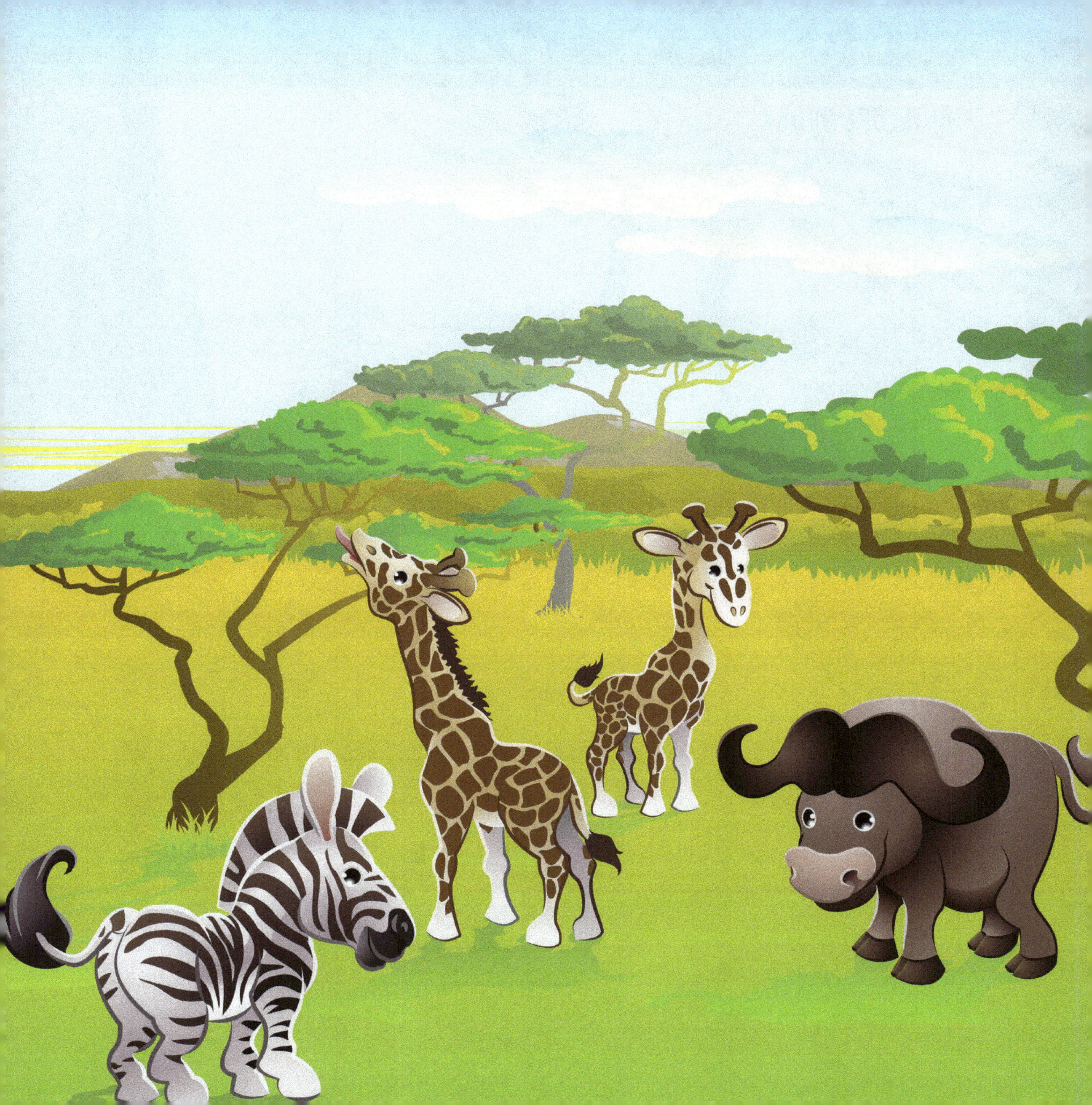

ANTELOPE ADDAX

ADDAX

The addax is a large antelope whose coat is light brown in summer and sort of gray in winter. They have white legs and white marks on their faces. They can survive extreme heat, so they can live in the desert as well as in the savanna.

AFRICAN BUFFALO

BUFFALO

Water buffalo spend most of their time in the water of lakes and rivers, eating plants and keeping cool.

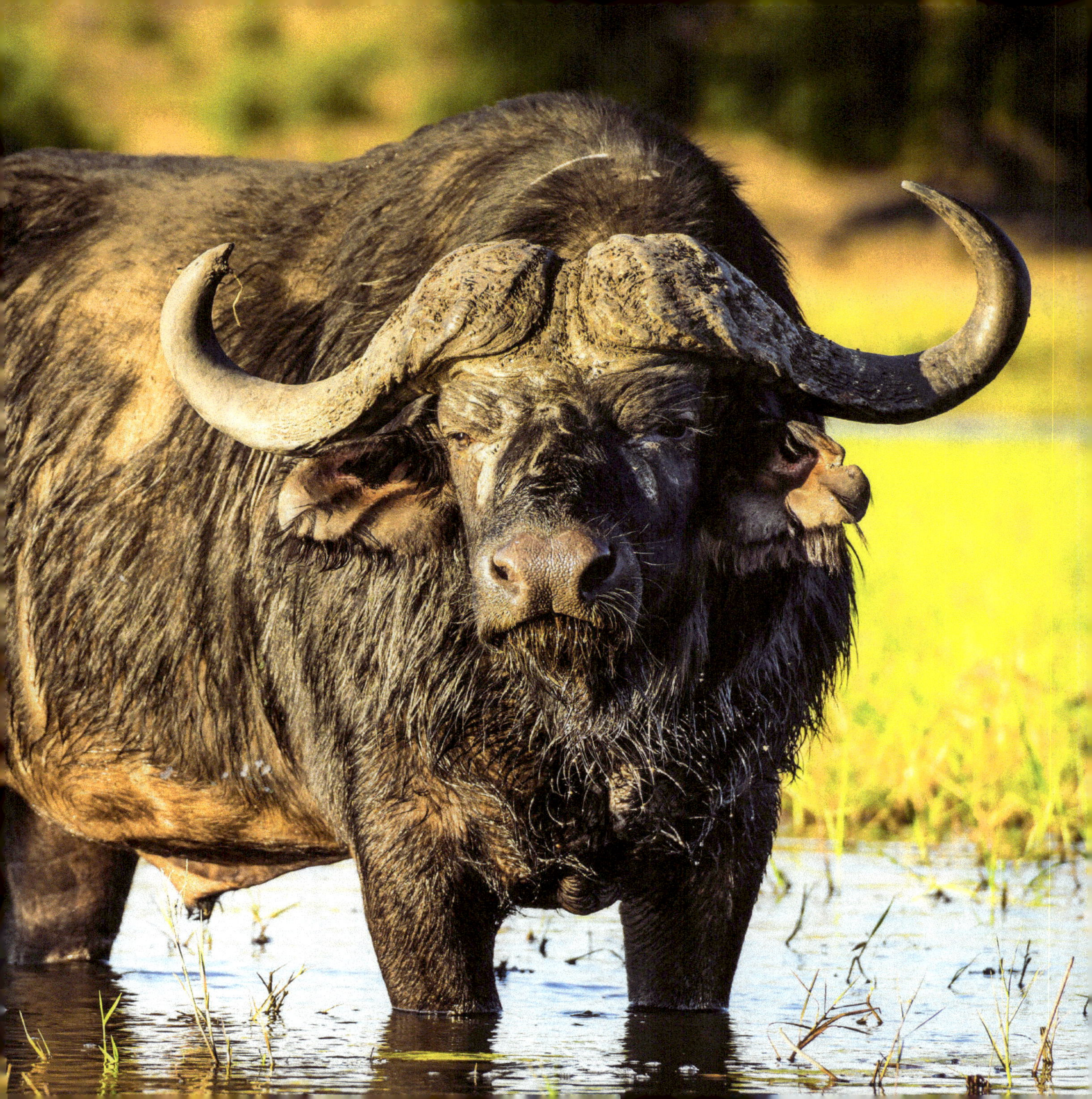

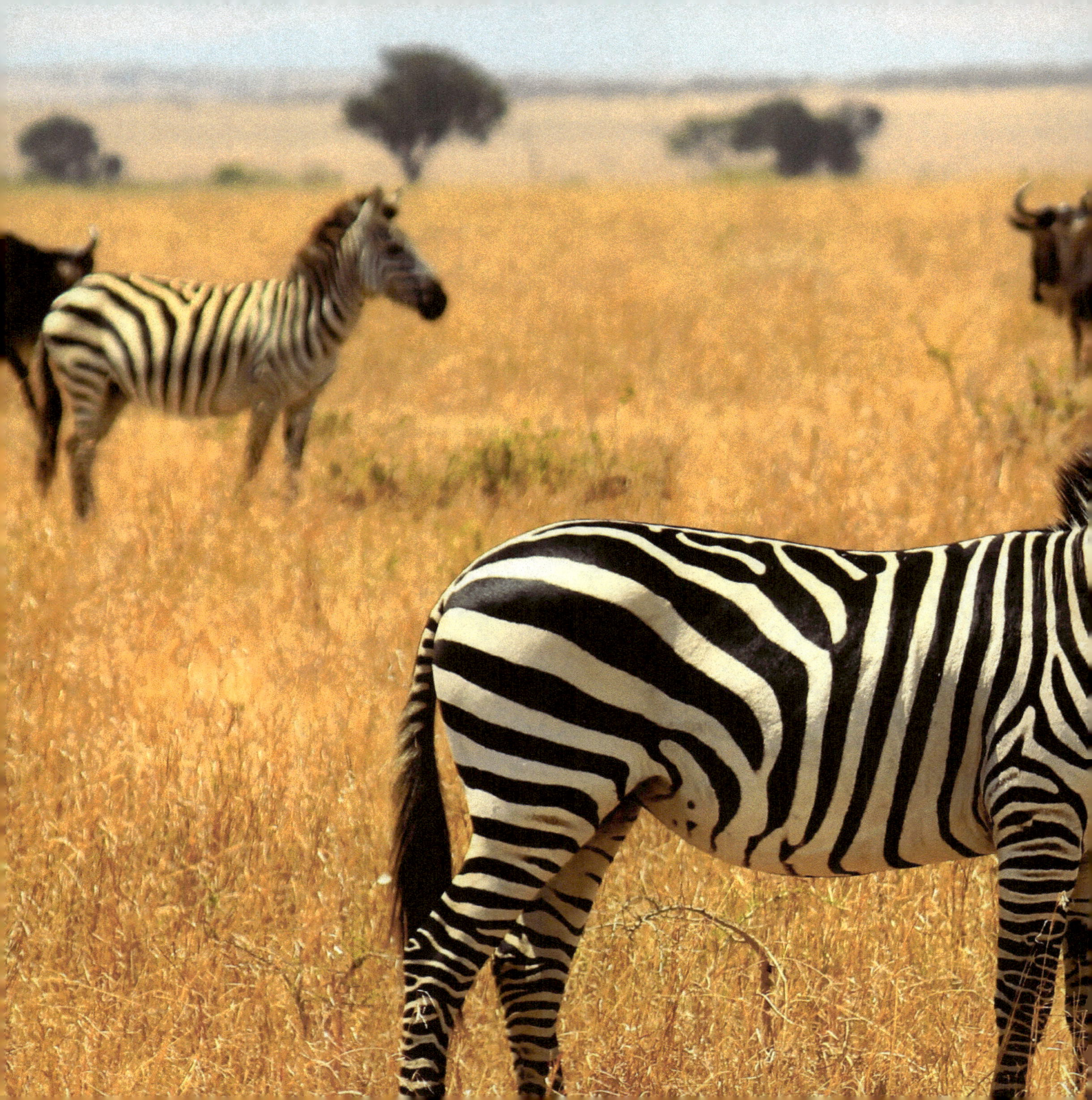

ZEBRA

ZEBRA

Zebras wear stripes of white and black on their bodies. This camouflage confuses hunters who want to chase them, because it is harder to see how fast the zebra is moving, and how far away it is.

DIK-DIK

DIK-DIK

These antelopes get their name from the sound they make when they are worried or afraid. They are grey-brown and have a tuft of hair on the top of their heads. The male dik-diks have short horns hidden in that hair!

LARGE MALE ELAND ANTELOPE

ELAND

These large antelopes can weigh as much as a ton. They can run and jump very well, which helps them get away when they are attacked.

ELEPHANT

AFRICAN ELEPHANT

The elephants of Africa have large ears that they use to protect their shoulders and upper bodies from the sun. They have strong trunks and long tusks, and are very smart. Elephants have good memories of places, people, and events, and are good parents to their children.

IMPALA

Impalas are great jumpers. They can do a thirty-foot long jump. They are red-brown on their backs and white on their bellies.

IMPALA

WALLER'S GAZELLE

WALLER'S GAZELLE

The Waller's Gazelle has a long neck, small head, and large ears. The males have horns and strong necks so they can fight with the horns when they need to. They are also called the Gerenuk Gazelle.

GIRAFFE

Giraffes are the tallest animals now living, although some dinosaurs from long ago were taller. They have long tongues that are good at grasping and pulling food they want to eat. They look peaceful, but adult giraffes will even fight a lion to defend their babies. They can kick very hard, and if the lion is not careful, it will be sorry it ever thought of bothering a giraffe.

A MOTHER GIRAFFE WITH HER BABY.

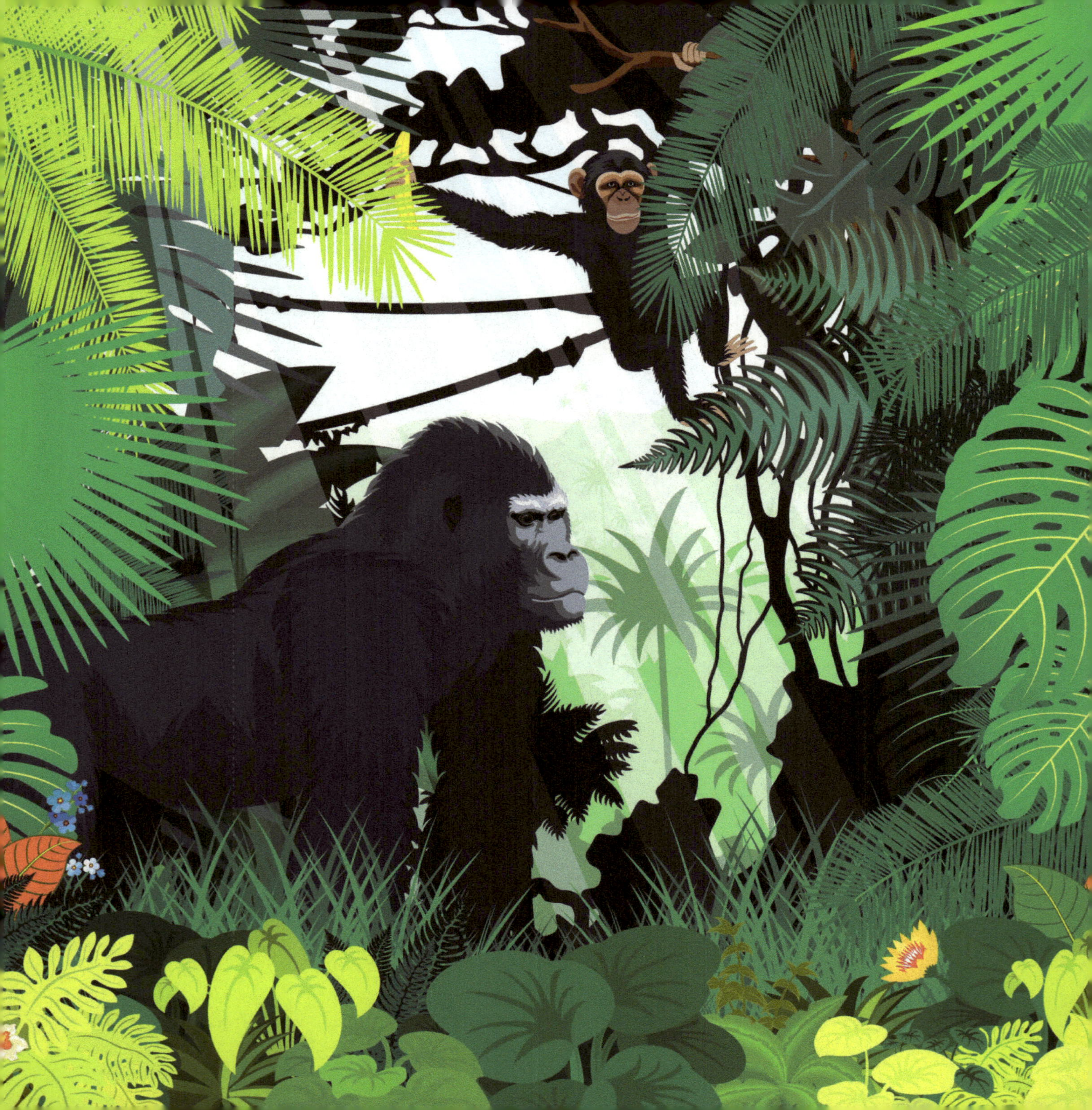

PRIMATES

The most successful primates of the African savanna evolved into humans! Human beings started in Africa and then slowly migrated to live and develop in almost every part of the world.

Here are two of our primate cousins of the savanna:

BABOON

Baboons spend a lot of their time in the forests, but they also visit and look for food and water in the savanna. They live on the ground in large groups called troops. They are mainly plant-eaters, but they will also make a meal of insects, fish, small birds, and small mammals like rabbits and even the smallest types of antelopes.

CUTE BABOON SITTING ON A BRANCH

MALE PATAS MONKEY SITTING ON A ROCK

PATA

Patas live on the ground in the savanna and can run very fast. They are the fastest of all the primates. They also have a very long tail.

OTHERS

Here are some other savanna dwellers. There are many more, too!

AARDVARK

Aardvarks live all over Africa. They have a sticky tongue with which they pull termites out of their nests. They see really poorly, but they have very strong legs and claws for digging. This helps them open up the termite nests.

AARDVARK

BAT-EARED FOX CUB

BAT-EARED FOX

As you can guess from their name, these little foxes have huge ears. They can spread their ears out to release excessive body heat, and this helps keep them cool. They eat termites, grasshoppers, scorpions, lizards and, when they can find them, fruit and eggs.

BUSHPIG

BUSHPIG

The bushpig looks like a pig you might find on any farm. It has small eyes with pale eyelashes, ears with tufts on the ends and a snout that has a blunt end. Bushpigs spend the day looking for things to eat, both vegetation like roots or the crops people have planted, and even small animals.

CIVET

The civet has a long, cat-like body with a long, furry tail. It has a white face and dark markings around their eyes it looks like a burglar. They live as much as they can in the trees. They have a strong smell, so sometimes people say they are the skunks of Africa.

CIVET

RHINOCEROS

There are five species of rhinoceros, but three of them are in danger of becoming extinct. People hunt them for their horns, which some people believe can be made into a powerful medicine. Rhinos mainly eat grass, buds from trees, fruit, leaves, and whatever they can find to chew on the tough bushes of the savanna. They are very aggressive and very near-sighted, which is not a good combination. They can sometimes charge toward what seems to be an enemy, but is only a cloud shadow. They sometimes fight with elephants, and have been known to attack cars and even trains.

A WHITE RHINO / RHINOCEROS

PANGOLIN

Pangolins eat ants. They have a long, sticky tongue that they slide down into an ant nest and bring back up all covered with wriggling ants to eat for supper. They have no teeth. To defend themselves, they have hard scales on their body. When they are attacked, they can roll into a ball of armor that most predators cannot break into.

PANGOLIN

GENET

GENET

Genets look like cats, but they are not part of the cat family. They have ringed tails, spots on their coat, big ears, and a small head. They eat other small creatures, hunting at night, and leave a strong-smelling musk to mark their territory and keep rival genets away.

GERBIL

Gerbils are like mice or hamsters. They are small and furry, and have a long tail. If an attacker grabs a gerbil by the tail, the gerbil can just release the tail and run away. It can grow a new tail later. They live underground, and have sharp claws for digging.

GERBIL

DUIKER

Duiker are antelopes, but unlike the others they mainly live by themselves instead of in herds. They blend into the land very well so it is hard to spot them. Their front legs are shorter then their hind legs so they look like they are tilted forward. They don't just eat grass, but eat bark, seeds, leaves, insects, and even rodents and small birds.

DUIKER

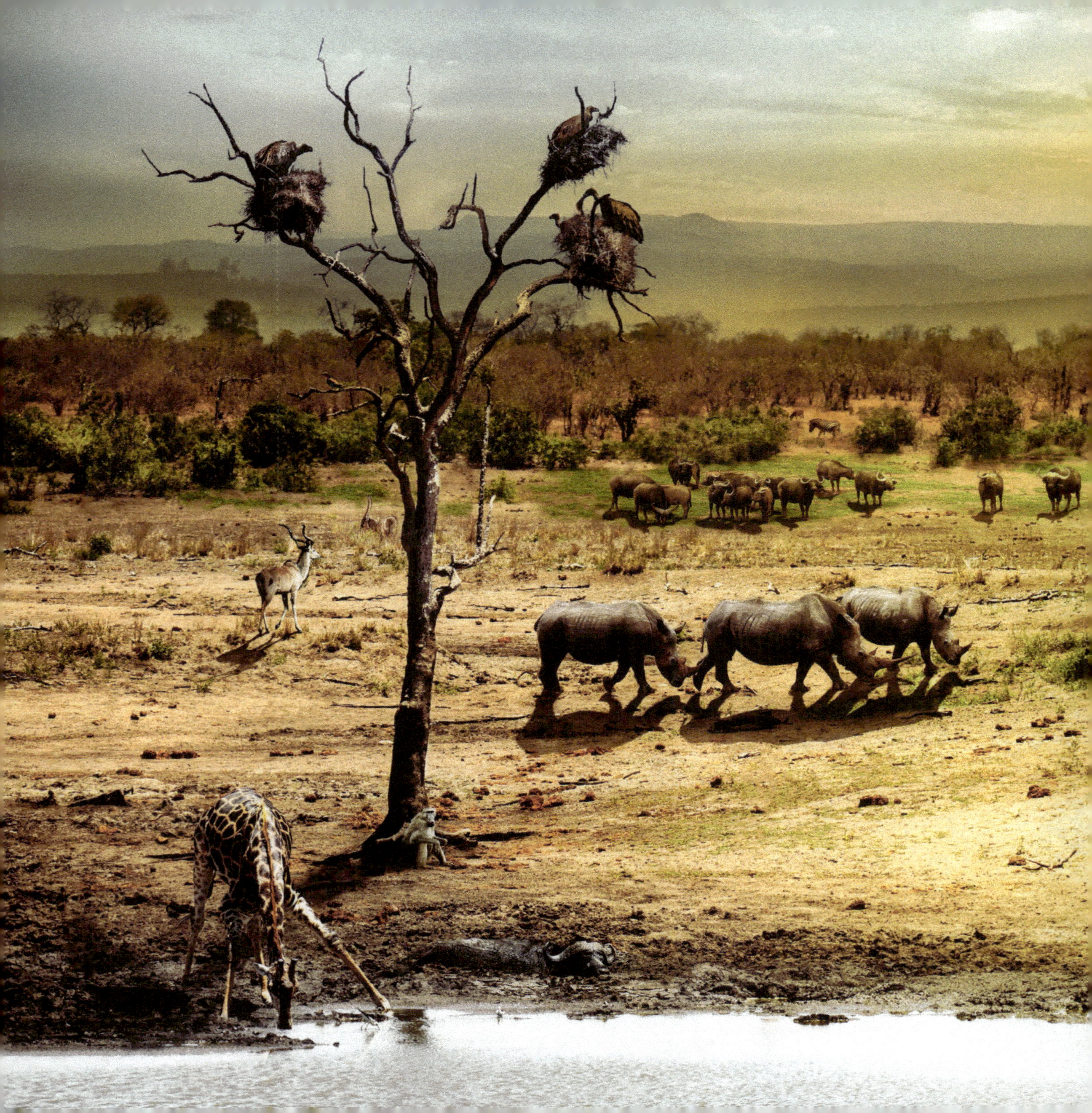

A LIVELY WORLD

Animals live all over this world! Find out about others in Baby Professor books like My Pet Cat Has Wild Cousins, Penguins Like Warm Climates, Too!, and The Great White Shark.

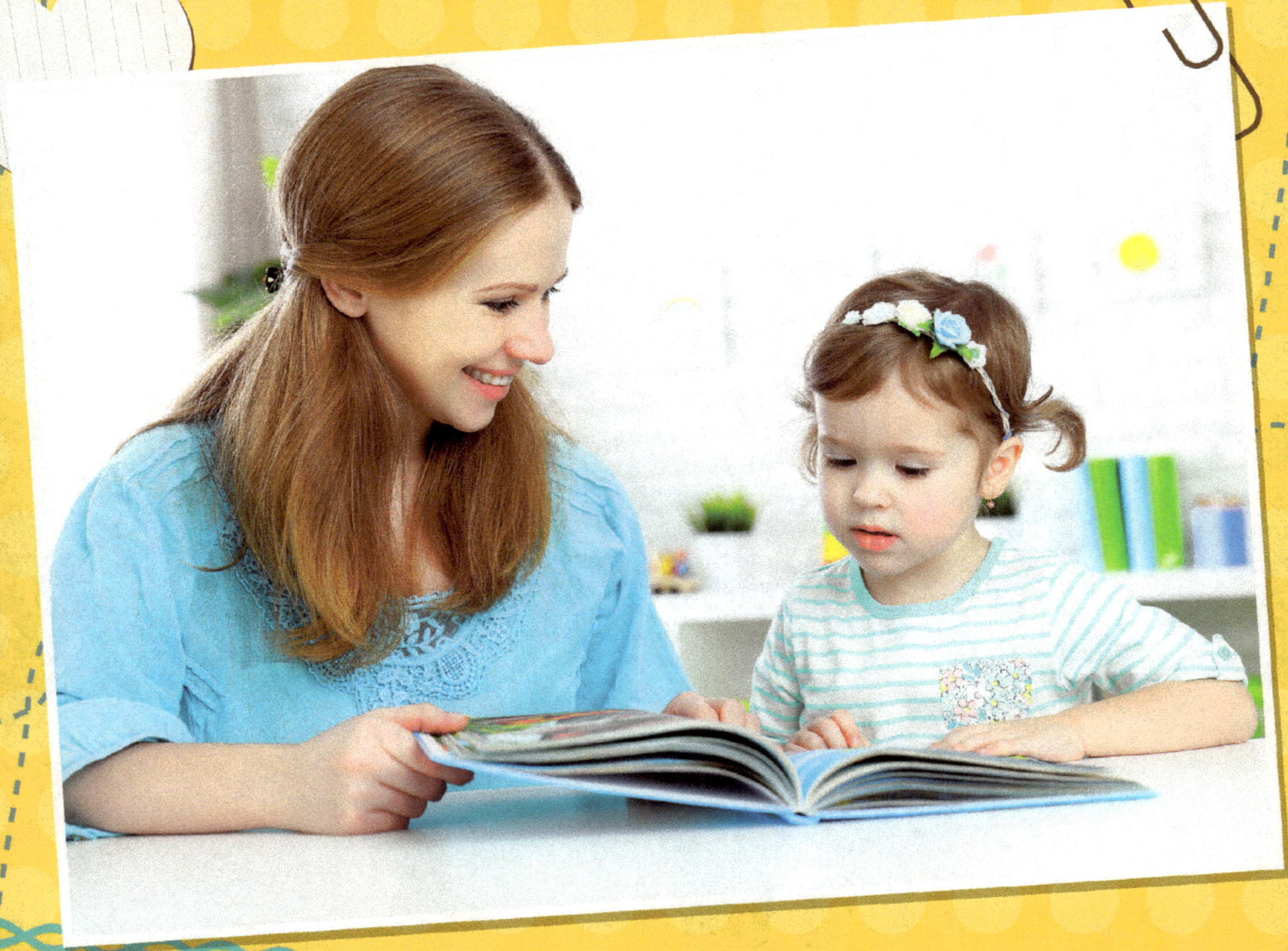

Visit

BABY PROFESSOR
EDUCATION KIDS

www.BabyProfessorBooks.com

to download Free Baby Professor eBooks and view our catalog of new and exciting Children's Books